Tefo and the Lucky Football Boots

by Lauri Kubuitsile

illustrated by Moni Perez

CAMBRIDGE
UNIVERSITY PRESS

In association with

Institute of Education

Chapter 1

One day, Omar was in school with his friends Tefo and Pelo. They saw Mr Mars put up a notice.

'I think that notice is for the football team,' Omar said. 'Let's go and check.'

Tefo read the notice. 'Come to the trials for the Lions football team on Friday. Only two people will be picked.'

'Oh no! But all three of us love football,' Omar groaned.

'Well, only two of us can get in the team. Let the best boys win!' Pelo said.

Tefo hoped Mr Mars would pick him. He wanted to be in the Lions football team. He loved football more than anything. But Omar and Pelo were also very good players. What could he do?

Tefo needed to talk to Grandpa about this. Long ago, Grandpa was a famous footballer. He scored many goals for his team. He was also very wise. He would know what to do to help Tefo get a place in the Lions.

Grandpa was happy to see Tefo. 'Why are you visiting me today, Tefo?' he asked.

'Grandpa, I need help. I want to get a place in the football team, but the other boys are very good,' Tefo said. 'I'm afraid that I am not good enough.'

'I know just what you need,' Grandpa said.

He went to another room and came back with a pair of football boots. They were old and dirty.

'What are those?' Tefo asked.

'These are my lucky football boots. When I was your age, I wore them and I got in the football team. They will help you too,' said Grandpa, handing him the boots. But could these boots really help Tefo?

Chapter 2

'Okay boys, I want you to show me how well you can play,' Mr Mars said. 'Get out on the field!'

'Good luck!' Tefo said to Omar and Pelo.

Pelo looked at Tefo's old, dirty boots.

'You are going to need a lot of luck with
those old boots,' he said.

Pelo laughed. But Tefo didn't care. He knew
the boots were lucky. He knew they would help
him get in the team.

Pelo was the goalkeeper. The whistle blew and
the boys began to play. One kicked the ball to Tefo.
He ran fast. Two boys tried to take the ball, but
Tefo ran faster. Faster and faster he went.
They could not stop him. And Tefo knew why.
It was the boots! His lucky boots!

Tefo kicked the ball. Whoosh! It flew straight past
Pelo and into the net!

'Come!' Mr Mars shouted. The boys gathered around him. 'I have chosen the two boys who will join the Lions. They are Pelo and Tefo!'

'Well done, Tefo,' said Omar, even though he was disappointed.

Would Tefo keep playing so well now he was in the team?

Chapter 3

Tefo was so happy. Now he was part of the Lions.

'Well played, Tefo,' said Pelo. He shook Tefo's hand. 'But you should buy a new pair of boots before the game,' he said.

Tefo said nothing. He would never get rid of his lucky football boots.

Tefo played very well in the next game. He won the ball from the other team four times. He scored a goal in the first half.

The game was nearly over. Tefo had the ball and – whoosh! In it went. He scored another goal and the Lions won the game.

'You're one of our best players,' Mr Mars said. 'Keep it up, Tefo!'

HOME 3 AWAY 1

13

Tefo was very happy. He loved football and now his dream was real. He was playing in a football team and he was one of the best players! Was he playing well because of his lucky football boots?

Chapter 4

Two weeks later, the Lions were going to play the Strikers. The Strikers were a very good team. Tefo was excited.

He looked everywhere for his lucky football boots, but he could not find them.

'Mama, have you seen my boots?' he asked.

'You mean those old dirty ones?' asked Mama.

'Yes,' Tefo said.

'I threw them away. I bought you these lovely new boots instead,' Mama said.

'Threw them away? Where?' Tefo asked.

'In the big dustbin downstairs,' Mama said.

Tefo rushed outside. He checked the dustbin.
The football boots were not there!

Tefo jumped on his bike and rode to the rubbish dump. When he arrived, the gates were locked.

A man saw Tefo. He came over and said, 'You are too late. We are closed.'

Tefo was very sad. Without his lucky football boots, he would not play well. Without his lucky football boots, the team might lose. What could he do?

Chapter 5

There was nothing Tefo could do. He had to get to the game. He put on the new football boots.

On the field, the Strikers were very fast. Tefo tried to run fast and catch them, but he could not.

Finally, Tefo got the ball. He began to run. 'Faster,' he said to himself. 'Faster, faster.' Suddenly, he tripped and fell. A player from the Strikers took the ball and scored a goal. The Lions were losing!

A boy from the other team ran past with the ball. Oh no! The Strikers might get another goal.

Tefo forgot about the boots. He had to help his team.

Tefo started to run. In a flash he caught up with the boy and took the ball. He ran faster and faster. The net was close. Tefo kicked the ball hard.

'Goal!' cheered his friends.

Soon, Tefo scored again. The Lions won!

My new boots might be lucky too, he thought.

After the game, Grandpa waited for Tefo.

'Well done, Tefo. One day you will be a better player than me,' Grandpa said.

'But I wasn't wearing your lucky football boots,' Tefo said.

Grandpa smiled and said, 'You never needed lucky boots, Tefo. You are a great player!'

Tefo and the Lucky Football Boots — Lauri Kubuitsile

Teaching notes written by Sue Bodman and Glen Franklin

Using this book

Developing reading comprehension

This is a story in the series about Omar and his friends from the International School strand of the Cambridge Reading Adventures. Children who have read the earlier stories will be familiar with the characters and settings. There are time shifts in the story which adds to the complexity of comprehension required. This is supported well by the illustrations. The book is organised in five short chapters to support sustained reading at this band.

Grammar and sentence structure

- Time connectives portray the events over time.
- A range of simple and complex sentence structures used for impact and effect.
- Paragraphing supports organisation of ideas.

Word meaning and spelling

- Literary-style devices, such as sound effects (e.g. 'whoosh' on page 12,) and phrases (e.g. 'Faster and faster he went' on page 9) are evident.
- Longer, more complex words (e.g. 'everywhere', 'without') are read using syllabification and known reading vocabulary.

Curriculum links

Social Science – Children could explore their own family history, and find out about what their grandparents did when they were younger.

Literacy – What are the children's aspirations for what they want to be when they grow up?

Learning Outcomes

Children can:

- read through longer passages of text in paragraphs, sustaining meaning as they read
- monitor their own reading for accuracy and comprehension
- read more complex words using known vocabulary.

A guided reading lesson

Book Introduction

Give each of the children a book. Ask them to read the title and blurb quietly to themselves. Point out that this story is in chapters. *Today, in guided reading, we will be reading the first four chapters. You will be able to read the last chapter on your own independently when we have finished working together.*

Orientation

Discuss other titles in this series that the children may have read previously (e.g. Omar Can Help, or Omar in Trouble). Say: *This is another story in the same series. This time it is about Tefo. What other characters do you know?*

Ask: *You have all read the blurb. What will the story be about, do you think?* Take some ideas.

Preparation

Page 3: Take the children to the dilemma – there are only two places available on the team for the three friends. Who will be chosen?

Page 4: Draw the children's attention to the picture. What is this indicating? (i.e. that this is a time in the past). Ask: *Can you quickly look at the text and find out something important about Tefo's grandfather. Yes, he was a famous football player when he was*